Spectral Realms

No. 19 ‡ Summer 2023

Edited by S. T. Joshi

The spectral realms that thou canst see
With eyes veil'd from the world and me.

H. P. LOVECRAFT, "To a Dreamer"

SPECTRAL REALMS is published twice a year by Hippocampus Press,
P.O. Box 641, New York, NY 10156 (www.hippocampuspress.com).
Copyright © 2023 by Hippocampus Press.
All works are copyright © 2023 by their respective authors.
Cover art and design by Daniel V. Sauer
Hippocampus Press logo by Anastasia Damianakos.

ISBN 978-1-61498-411-5   ISSN 2333-4215

Contents

Poems 5
  Tenebrae / Wade German 7
  The Monstrous Word Is "Man" / Carl E. Reed 8
  A Grave Vision / Scott J. Couturier 9
  The Remains / Patricia Dompieri 10
  Strange Door, Odd Key / Frank Coffman 12
  Interrupted / Lori R. Lopez 14
  Surviving Samhain / Andrew White 18
  North of Arkham / David Barker 19
  Genevieve and Amun / Alicia Hilton 20
  The Boneless / Leigh Blackmore 23
  Another Apocalypse / Lee Clark Zumpe 24
  Novembering / Ann K. Schwader 25
  The Darkest Days and Nights / Benjamin Blake 26
  The Nightmare / Geoffrey Reiter 27
  The Traveler / Ian Futter 28
  Witchbirds / Lori R. Lopez 30
  After Hesse / Don Webb 33
  The Myth of Nothing / Maxwell I. Gold 34
  Gods of the Garden / Steven Withrow 35
  The Phoenix / Ngo Binh Anh Khoa 36
  Pontianak / Christian Dickinson 37
  On *The Invitation*, an Anonymous Oil Seen in a Flea Market /
     Manuel Pérez-Campos 38
  The Cicada Kings / Joshua Green 39
  Frankenskin for Frankenbones / Oliver Smith 40
  Alanna / Garrett Boatman 42
  Mortality's Metronome / LindaAnn LoSchiavo 45
  Ancient Rite: A Walk amongst the Corn / Carl E. Reed 46
  Face Your Future / DJ Tyrer 48
  The Sorcerer in His Tower Contemplating Possible Success /
     Darrell Schweitzer 49
  Sycophant of the Siren / Jay Sturner 50
  Iron-Sceptred Skeleton / Dmitri Akers 52

Bone or Root / Denise Dumars 54
Language of Night / William Clunie 56
Brocéliande / Manuel Arenas 58
Boy Meets Girl / David C. Kopaska-Merkel 59
The Witch / Katherine Kerestman 60
The Last House / Jason Hardy 62
The Battlefield / Adam Bolivar 64
The End of Day / Ngo Binh Anh Khoa 65
A Cabin in the Wood / Frank Coffman 66
They're Coming / Maxwell I. Gold 69
On an Autumnal Graveyard / Scott J. Couturier 70
The Death of the Sculptor's Model / Steven Withrow 71
A Willing Sacrifice / Andrew White 72
Epiphany on the Bronze Poseidon at Cape Sounion /
   Manuel Pérez-Campos 73
Nuckelavee / Christian Dickinson 74
The Bayou / Lee Clark Zumpe 75
An Invitation / Claire Smith 76
Seer Light / Liam Garriock 78
The Machine / Ian Futter 80
By the Sea / David Barker 83
The Castle Beneath the Hedgerow / Silvatiicus Riddle 84
Small Doses / F. J. Bergmann 86
Christmas Lure / Alicia Hilton 88
The Lantern of September / Scott C. Couturier 90
The Ferryman's Rest / Joshua Green 92
In Medusa's Coils / DJ Tyrer 93
Lob / Frank Coffman 94
An Apostate's Eschatology / Carl E. Reed 97
Sphinx / Christian Dickinson 98
The Matron / Ngo Binh Anh Khoa 99
The Towers / Maxwell I. Gold 102
confession / Lee Clark Zumpe 103
Sympathy for Laocoön and His Sons / Manuel Pérez-Campos 104

Classic Reprints 105
    The Nightmare / Erasmus Darwin 107
    The Haunter / Thomas Hardy 109

Reviews 111
    An American Omar / S. T. Joshi 113

Notes on Contributors 117

Poems

Tenebrae

Wade German

Darkness brooded through the valley,
    Stars had heralded the night;
Ancient evening from the eons
    Raised its veil to raptured sight:
And its beauty was a vision
    Strange and glowing, ebon bright.

Then the shadowed earth fell silent,
    Muted, like a calm black sea;
Then the wave of starry ocean
    Washed its waveless world on me—
Breathless, I beheld in wonder,
    As a newborn babe might see:

Saw the Darkness for one Spirit,
    Heard its prayer of voiceless verse:
Beckoning all worlds, all Being,
    Down black gulfs and there immerse . . .
Darkness holy, holy, holy,
    Darkness weaved the universe.

The Monstrous Word Is "Man"

Carl E. Reed

The monstrous word is "man," not ghoul or ghost:
a beast unleashed by circumstance & fate
to rampage 'cross the world in killing hosts
murdering for god, king & nation state.
The monstrous word is "man," not undead corpse
arisen stiff-limbed, moaning from the grave;
in blighted cities, towns & stagnant thorpes
rabid apes mass in temple, mosque & nave.
The monstrous word is "man," not horned devil
slavering in some rutilant, hot hell;
thing of rage, mad lusts & madder revels:
mankind!—by whims & grim fancies impelled.
Cynical pinnacle of green-grassed Earth:
creature of joyous sorrows & black mirth.

A Grave Vision

Scott J. Couturier

There came upon me a transporting vision—
Of autumn foliage robing an ancient grave,
coffin's shape traced beneath red-litten loam.
I beheld myself sealed deep belowground,
my own hands crossed on stillness of breast,
a pale face that could attest to too many days
spent away from the sun: an unmade self,
graven in & consigned to clay, with eyes
made to stare ever-upwards towards worlds
by all flesh forsaken. A still, silent shell
in a hole, draped over with shriveled foliate
bouquets which skitter & rasp, whisper & dance,
crimson demons weaving spells atop my stone
even as entropy molders & wastes to bone:

Then, the vision forsook my wondering sight,
leaving only leaves scattered, & a tomb blanched white.

The Remains

Patricia Dompieri

The air is stagnant; oppressive.
The dark earthy scent wafts through the air.
Dust particles float listlessly in the blinding sunbeams that creak through the rotting boards.
In the dim, moldy, cavernous space, where darkness contrasts with the noonday sun, oblong boxes, trunks and corrugated cardboard containers are haphazardly stacked in neglected cobwebbed corners.
Unwholesome seepage stains the floors, darkened black pools of tainted liquefied muck,
An eerie warehouse; these strange boxes containing corpses of various states of decay,
abandoned, without explanation, nor answers.
Freshly, unearthed ground, in mountainous heaps,
as a quiet, forgotten, condemned, forlorn community coughs up its dead.
Every standing structure, converted to a grim warehouse.
Bodies slick, bloated and pungent,
corpses leathered and petrified,
remains dry, parched, withered, brittle, and decomposed.
Remains, lifeless shells, empty husks, chaff,
in pieces,
rests.
Dust particulates drift aimlessly,
a flakey layer of soot,

slowly swirling, falling downwards, down to rest
an eerie snowfall
coats the yellowed window pane.
Everything is buried with
Bone and dust—
only remains,
rest in pieces . . .

Strange Door, Odd Key

Frank Coffman

Ah! They have found it!—one of many portals.
But this one gate was closed long years ago,
Hidden among the refuse that these mortals
Accumulate, store away, or idly throw
As trash—*or* simply forget amidst the attic's mess—
As this one, long since lost—now rediscovered.
They do not ken that I may gain access
Into their world, nor do they know I've hovered
Near this old passage since I last went through
Into their world. *For what are fifty years to Me?*
Those who now occupy the house are new.
As tenants come and go there have been three
Groups of humans living in this place
Since those foolish warm ones opened wide the door.
How delicious was the fear upon each face,
When they beheld me in their abject horror!

Yes! Now these new ones start to work at *spells*,
Asking their inane questions as they begin,
Not knowing that legions from the deepest Hells
Wait on this side *each* gate, yearn to go in.

In unison they ply their handiwork.
Soon they are asking what mortals should not know,
Not realizing I guide them, that I lurk
Behind the portal, that the things I show

Them are all meant to urge more queries, lure
Them to the questions that will open wide
This gateway. The words that will ensure
That I—now outside—am allowed *inside*
Their realm. "Is there someone here?" asks one.
I answer, "YES!" My passage coming near.
The other, "Are you human?" Answer: "NO!"
And then, "Will you give some sign or join us here?"
And with my "YES!" the threshold now is crossed,
Through plectrum's eye I glide and they are lost!
Like smoke I enter—then materialize!
Such terror! They cannot believe their eyes!
Their final cries resound in the room's gloom.
And, once again, the Ouija has led to doom.

Interrupted

Lori R. Lopez

I

Somebody died and left me adrift,
soon to be homeless, cast out and short-shrift,
according to the glaring red-letter decree
buried in mail sent by strangers to me.

I quit reading such things, a big waste of time!
The envelope unopened; it wasn't a crime.
Till finally a peek, invaders at the door—
I sank to my knees, then clung to the floor.

Where would I go? Whether living or dead,
I couldn't be certain the state of my head.
You suddenly realize how precious each drop
when it's down to a teacup once filled at the top,
but now lying empty, my lips dry as bone.
These walls were a bastion I dwelt in alone.

Hiding from barbarians who battered my gate,
come to clear what I strove to accumulate.
I railed at the rudeness of the quiet's disruption:
"Shatterers of peace, I'm no pest or corruption
to toss in the street, or fill a Dumptruck!"
One way or another, a deal had been struck.

II

Reduced to a closet, what little remained—
several boxes of belongings to which I was chained.
My spirit abandoned, I lingered unfinished,
desperate to hang on. Remembered yet diminished.

Fretting over tasks interrupted, incomplete;
dissatisfied I languished . . . undone, obsolete.
A sense of commitment still burning, abiding.
Forced to share my home with the person residing.

A niece scarcely known who inherited my lot,
and disposed of the bulk, even selling my plot
for a small pot of ashes stowed high on a shelf
in a tombish enclosure of coats and myself.
A few cartons and trunks, not much to my name.
The rest in a landfill—an absolute shame.

Being stored like an object, attached to this vault:
a knickknack or brickbrack, ignored by default.
Family Photographs spared. A jumble of Antiques.
Among hats and souvenirs, playing Hide-And-Seek,
standing in the dark near a dustpan and broom,
obnoxiously gagging on ghostly perfume.

III

A statue just staring at a door seldom budged,
the wood lacking grain, very plain, a bit smudged.
Petrified from boredom, having nothing else to do,
I tipped forward napping and toppled right through!

My house unfamiliar, all touches erased . . .
Inspecting the rooms I felt lost and replaced,
then noticed my pallor grown feeble with age.
How many calendars had turned every page?

The niece gathered wrinkles, gray in her hair.
I feared her the last who knew I'd been there,
and watched with alarm her life dwindle away,
balancing my fate on her plate day by day—
Carelessly unhealthy. Prone to disaster.
I didn't wish to fade out of sight any faster.

Refusing to go gently, I cracked the mirror
while trying to convey a message clearer.
Ruth hosted a séance, afraid she was haunted.
A medium pretended to guess what I wanted.
Midnight gonged. The niece clutched her heart.
Two kindred souls will both wane and depart . . .

IV

We the Dead watch the ones most connected,
who preserve our memories, our flames protected.
Good or bad, that love or loathing bond
crosses the Divide, bridging the Beyond.

Providing the glue, a deathline or tether
to pull us ashore from an ocean of nether,
else we must sink in Oblivion's dark sea,
the end that awaits us all eventually.

Remember. Do what you can to resist!
If you forget us or expire, we cease to exist.
Unless being famous enough to endure—
The greatest and worst are rarely obscure.

Surviving Samhain

Andrew White

Creatures exit from monstrous wombs
While spirits dance among the tombs.
Zombies feed and werewolves bite—
Samhain is their favorite night!

Specters haunt and vampires prowl,
Succubi stalk and banshees howl.
Danger is lurking all around—
Horrors of every sort can be found.

How will we make it through this alive?
The strong and the clever just might survive.
Don't forget a rune of protection
Lest you end up in a bone collection!

North of Arkham

David Barker

Near end of day I climb the rocky height
That gives a view of Innsmouth and its bay
Where ships arrive from South Seas ports each day,
Their lurid freight removed 'neath cloak of night.
Great casks of gold adornments hammered bright
Are rolled down ramps by those who lurch and bray
And into vaults where they are hid away
For order's sake, stored deep and out of sight.

As sunset comes and shadows flood the land,
I reach the peak and spy the ships at sea,
Their tattered sails unfurled for all to see—
By gill-necked crews these errant ships are manned.
Then down in Innsmouth, hordes of fish-folk stream
From ancient doors, a terrifying dream!

Inspired by H. P. Lovecraft's sonnet "VIII. The Port"
in *Fungi from Yuggoth*.

Genevieve and Amun

Alicia Hilton

Yard sales were dangerous.
Bad karma, broken dreams
and rusty metal lurked in bric-a-brac.
Genevieve shoved a skinny woman
with beady eyes like a vulture
and grasped the sarcophagus.
A dusty mummy case,
battered and surprisingly light,
but gold and enamel gleamed bright.

Genevieve swaddled the sarcophagus
in a tarp, hailed a taxi.
Someone die? the driver said.
She used a hex to wipe his memory.

Finally home in her London lair,
Genevieve set the sarcophagus on the bed.
Used a chisel to pry open the lid.
She chanted an incantation.
Dust swirled in the shape
of a malevolent face.
A mummy materialized.
Reanimated lips bared fangs
longer than her thumbs.

* * *

Amun suckled her flesh
while they fucked,
sealing their unholy pact,
mapping her body with fang marks.

Amun's thirst could not be quenched.
They hunted prey in libraries,
bit patrons and librarians,
draining their life essence
and wisdom.

Amun siphoned Genevieve's magic
whenever he feasted.
In thirty-two days,
her face aged a decade.
Bones become brittle.
Joints swelled with arthritis.

On New Year's Eve
Genevieve grabbed a knife
from their kitchen
while Amun slaughtered
Nazi zombies.
A reanimated prince
obsessed with video games.

*   *   *

Creeping on kitty cat feet,
she pounced and thrust the knife
with all her might,
severing undead muscles,
scraping a rib bone.

Amun howled like a banshee,
wrenched the blade from his chest,
skewered Genevieve's left eye.

The undead ancient one
inhaled her last breath,
gave her a sharp kiss
of immortality.

The sickle moon was waxing
when Genevieve wed Amun.
The vampire bride wore a black gown
and a scarlet eyepatch.

The Boneless

Leigh Blackmore

Slow-crawling things move strangely through the lanes
Of twisted towns sepulchral. Scorching fires
Illume dim ashen skies; curious strains
Of music, sung by townsfolk in weird choirs,

Rise forth to hold the rotting things at bay.
The monstrous creatures pay the songs no heed.
They slither forth, these boneless things of clay,
Like loathly worms with tongueless mouths—and feed

On humans they encounter as they roam.
Benighted blasphemies from black domains
Make leprous sojourn from their bestial home
And squirm across the vast and darkling plains . . .

Another Apocalypse

Lee Clark Zumpe

Surely you have seen the Signs—
the actualization of prophecies,
the meaning of which are so often
obscured until something happens
and we can piece it all together.

Surely you have heard the Word—
the gospel of cryptic poets
translated and propagated,
collected in esoteric scribbles
and now digitally disseminated.

Surely you believe the Truth—
the intimate horror we all cherish,
apocalyptic nightmares played out
in myth, cinema and dream,
the terrible fear we secretly desire.

Surely you will see the End—
when unseen forces shall intersect,
clearly orchestrated by dark designs,
ever gathering amongst the shadows
amidst inaccessible extinguished stars.

Novembering

Ann K. Schwader

The shadows have us now. These faded gray
& inkblood imitations of our lives
are all the year has left us. Far away,
another sun. A sky where azure thrives
like birdsong visible: no whetted knives
of wind against our faces, seeking bone
beneath emotion. Now the light survives
in moments brief as afternoons alone
among abandoned trees. Like leaves, we've flown
beneath our colors, drifted out of reach
of memory. Amnesia season. Known
in frost-worn summer tongues, we lack a speech
to redefine us. Silence & cold rain
efface last outlines. We are ghosts again.

The Darkest Days and Nights

Benjamin Blake

Revelling in early mornings with the glorious whores
Ingesting a plethora of poison.
Losing the inner-self in animalistic rite
Blood-soaked dance floors of penultimate sin
And hands of fire.

The weakened son
Stumbles through streets of perpetual headache.
With forgotten sigils
Carved in books, bound in flesh.
An insatiable appetite
For what lurks upon the stairs.
Unknowingly knowing
The invitation
Sent through spritely eyes.

O, entropic desire
How much longer
'til these city walls crumble and fall
Into a crimson ocean, choked with lost limbs
Severed from slack-jawed saints,
And stuttering sinners?

The Nightmare

Geoffrey Reiter

Within the nightmare, all the dark congeals
Around our hearts and guts. We feel the falling,
The futile, flailing plunge to the appalling
Abyss. The night alight with monsters steals
Into our souls. Aghast, our courage reels,
And from the frantic fear within us crawling
We scuttle off to flee the fatal mauling,
And, caterwauling wildly, loose the seals
Of our souls' sanctum, huddling in this vault
That shall ensconce our selves. We slam the door
Secure in thunder, safe from harm and free
From fear. But in this bright-lit crypt we halt—
A shadow grows and glowers on the floor:
We are the deathly dream from which we flee.

The Traveler

Ian Futter

Alone, on the moon,
I ventured back
into the past,
and every scene was barren;
just as barren as the last.

All the countless cracks and craters,
formed in angry aeons past,
were but battered
nests to nothing;
nothing sheltered 'neath the blast.

No creatures craned round craggy cliffs
to watch my pointless plight.
No ancient eyes,
from deepest pit
did share my endless night.
Tiresome travels,
wearied wonders,
Ceaseless journeys, without end,
Teaming visions, dreams incessant,
Held no mark of foe or friend.

So I collapsed
upon the dust
and gazed into the sky.

A trillion winking, lonely lights
and rocks that cannot die
gazed blankly back upon me
as I lay amongst the sand,
and nothing moved
to still my storm
or hold my homeless hand.

It was then I felt a shudder;
shakes and shifts
beneath the ground.
A shocking scream,
which mocked my own
was echoing around.

A figure vast and formless
blocked my view
of stars and space,
and as it sensed my loss and fear
It laughed into my face.

Witchbirds

Lori R. Lopez

A stooped Beldam toils as her pot of stew boils.
Muttering and chanting, she stirs the soup ranting,
greedy cackle-breaths wishing lovely little deaths!
Eager to devour chubby cherubs sweet or sour.

Griselda, the Tor Hag, lives tilted on a crag,
brewing up potions from a Grimoire of notions
to perform a spelling blitz, catch kiddies in her mitts;
bind cats and mice in kind to a cunning woman's mind.

Umbral wingers are her faves, cooked rabidly in waves,
the cauldron all abubble, just a dash of oil and trouble—
a batch of Skull-Faced Moth, a frothy Witchbird broth:
for flights of ill portent; incantations of torment.

Cast into rampant night, full of devilry and fright . . .
batlike Crows throng home to be poured out of gloam,
while Jackdaws stray far from kettle and jar—
ingredients most fowl, born of feather and scowl.

Shadow-plumed, hearts afire, caws piercing the briar,
back to liquid Familiars fly; in dark glass they would lie,
yet each bottle of spilled ink may release a black drink
like a Jinn slightly crumpled, its quills a bit rumpled.

Keen squawks to be told, the voice of a scold—
rather grumpy in tights, complaining about Rights;
taking bites without teeth, scouring village and heath,
prone acerbically to rail at the twitch of a tail.

Always ready to brood, be plunged in a mood,
contrarily askew, with the temper of a Shrew.
Primed to pounce or denounce in the wink of a flounce
that gruesome gnarled biddy. Not one drop of pity!

How callous both sides steeped in flagrant derides.
Not all Crones think alike, some as cruel as a Shrike.
But ladybirds are picky, not to mention quite tricky,
and the company they keep runs immeasurably deep.

Calling all of them pets, the Hag wields pointed threats
against any who shunned her; townsfolk who wonder
if she is to blame for misfortunes and shame!
Griselda coos and charms, whispering grave harms.

"Witchbirds come alive! A flock of eight and five
must swoop down the slope, rudely steal away hope,
as I lure the plump darlings collected like Starlings
to feather my nest—young blood to ingest!"

The one-woman Coven gaily lights a large oven,
then sharpens her knives for chopping up lives.
A Corvus objects; an aggrieved Rook protects
a delirious childling plucked aloft like a wild thing.

From talons the girl hung. Lindy-Sue calmly swung,
delivered by a Jailbird, a clang of iron heard.
Down dives stoic Mooneye, as mad as a Magpie—
a razor-rimmed hailstone splitting open the Crone.

When babies are freed, the Crows have no need
cramming Inkwells or Jams for penning Hexagrams.
A murder-mob inserts Baked Mistress for desserts.
No longer mass-produced, Witchbirds rule the roost.

After Hesse

Don Webb

My favorite story was the Prodigal Son:
He had all the tastes of evil, the wine, the women,
Yet all the celebrations of good—
The clean linen, the well-washed hands.
And everyone made a fuss
As I grew the idea of the taste of evil grew:
The magic, the other worlds, the things glimpsed in dreams;
Then blood and things not easily named.
I threw myself into my damnation imagining my return,
But I forgot the well-washed hands, the clean linen
The light
I forgot even human
And now I love and lust with the ghoul pack
Having seen the ONE there is no turning back.

The Myth of Nothing

Maxwell I. Gold

Long before cities spread across the rock and cracked skin of that sad, lonely planet, there existed a crawling flesh, some mass of something or *other*. I was bled entirely of truth and meaning, left inside some cosmic sack of nothingness held within the last fragments of a world caught between the aftermath of yesterday and tomorrow. Too long did I wonder why they left us, left me here to wither betwixt flesh and shadow.

Marble graves and bone-colored temples build in horrid homage to the history I'd never understand, littered the burnt woods with stumps and stones like shriveled corpses, the last reminders that Nothing might never tread its feet upon this charred soil, ever again. *Were they mine? The graves, the temples?* My history or my curse, I'd never know, but they were there to torture me until the stars themselves fell at my side in fiery oblivion.

Still, I knew no answers would come, only the embittered starlight which hung low in the fog and murk of the new days continually haunted my tired brain. Their spectral songs pulled me ever closer towards that which was unthinkable, but ever desirable compared to my Promethean suffering. And every night, the music rose like the putrid waters of the salt-boiled oceans, revelations, and regret that *I was Nothing*. Reminders of the scorched earth and plastic fields whose glass tree now grew where no tree would ever grow, no beast dare to travel; except the ghost who desperately roamed the forsaken world, bled dry of truth, tossed in a sack of nothingness. He was Nothing. I was Nothing.

Gods of the Garden

Steven Withrow

Gods of the garden are growing thin,
And no one knows how long this night
Or nightmare may emaciate them further.
Dawn, in truth, was due eleven days ago,
But who has seen the sun, our sleeping star?
The first to feel night's scythe was Feverfew,
The deity of daisies, then Daffodil,
Whose yellow bulbs have blanched,
Her flower-faces furred with fungus now.
Roots are more resilient, and the steady rain
Is soaking succor for them. Still,
To live they must have light, or all is leaf-fall
And petal-plummeting. We pray for morning,
Hoping against hope doomed Hollyhocks will heal.

The Phoenix

Ngo Binh Anh Khoa

So rarely have the eyes of mortals gazed
Upon the fabled Phoenix soaring through
The star-filled night. Majestic was the view
Where pinions of bright gold and crimson blazed,
And where its wings—clasped by the vibrant teeth
Of flames—flew past, a trail of scorching fire
Ignited till it perched and built a pyre
On earth. Right then, how we forgot to breathe
As its own flames reduced its regal plume
To ashes. Haunting were the shrieks that shook
The heavens; silence henceforth overtook
The land, but from the remnants of its doom,
A rainbow-crested bird would then arise
And rend the pregnant stillness with its cries
As it reigned, glorious midst the dawn-lit skies.

Pontianak

Christian Dickinson

I scent men's flesh upon the moonlight breeze;
A hunger goads the frenzy in my mind.
One wanders through the forest, drunken-blind.
I sight my prey and leap from fruit-hung trees.

A maiden of the village once I was,
By all the men accounted wondrous fair;
One night did they my maidenhead forswear,
And give my vengeful spirit proper cause.

My nails drip blood as I begin the feast—
The heart—a most delectable repast;
The kidneys and the bladder next will serve;
But lungs and eke the stomach I reserve.
The liver, drenched in rum, I finish last,
And leave the corpse a warning—gently fleeced.

On *The Invitation,* an Anonymous Oil Seen in a Flea Market

Manuel Pérez-Campos

Its effulgence exudes through every variation
of its master tint a nocturne of spectral
decrepitude: next to a sleep-conquered
waterfront backed by hummingbird-haunted
acreage and circumscribed by a road
of green mud-encrusted macadam stands
proudly like a lost axiom amid strange
hybrids of carnivorous flora and mongrel
caterpillars which proliferate on the margins
an anorexic bride in long-sleeved white
cothardie, and over flaxen hair anademe
of gypsophila, her eyes sunken by old sins
of the flesh and as edgy as though about
to volatilize into ill-omened perfume
extending her blistered hand to someone
outside the frame: a bizarre queen proposing
to a spectator, for whom she has waited
innumerous lunations, and whose inmost darkness
she is, the spiritual drama of an especial
hierogamos, that they may exchange places.

The Cicada Kings

Joshua Green

I looked within the forest gleaming, soil
Unpacked from years of only silent wings.
For no thing crept under the boughs, no toil
Of ants lurking on old cicada kings.
I listened for those blaring tymbal rings,
Descending wooded paths until I found
An awful place where lords would chant by springs,
Their bodies splayed, forlorn on ancient ground.
I wondered, then, if they had once been crowned,
These ten-foot beasts, worshipped by men of old,
Unholy creatures bound by constant sound
But doomed to quietness by northern cold.
My weary eyes gave way to fear of death,
For even kings cannot command their breath.

Frankenskin for Frankenbones

Oliver Smith

It lay askew on the bench, an unfilled suit;
arm-bag, leg-bag, body-bag, and head-bag.
I became a tailor to sew this garment
of fine man-hide; spun sinew, twisted
needle-fine. I perforated the dermis
to seam and fit this empty, yellow body

with its veinous mottling, its buttonhole-eyes,
its scalp; purple-grained and crimson-threaded.
I lined its greenish flank with silk, so it
might wrap and snugly fit the naked organs;
capillaries crazy-quilted the spare rib
of my monstrously mis-sized new-Adam.

I wondered, should I use more boning
on the thorax or stumpwork on the limbs?
Appliqué on the belly? Charm-squares over spine?
The whole wonderous outfit I stitched;
trotter to snout, brisket to silverside, folded about
my mosaic écorché so recently ungraved.

Guts and muscles filled the patchwork dress
of grey, unliving gooseflesh. Tied off,
my grave-wax mannequin reposed, almost
ready for life, decanted like new wine into
an old skin; a wardrobe of old rags unpicked
and sewn to snuggly clothe these borrowed bones.

Alanna

Garrett Boatman

Alanna, maid of dark-brown hair,
    Hums a mournful tune
As treads her foot a measure sad
    Beneath a misty moon;
A cavern she her bower makes
Upon a cairn of dark-green lakes.

Alanna counts the countless stars
    And plucks the wild red rose;
The moon she watches wane and wax;
    The misty heather blows;
And with her slender bow of yew
She chases deer through evening dew.

But as a hare 'fore moor-fire flees,
    She flies before the day,
And hiding in her stony bower
    She sings a doleful lay;
Her fingers doth her harp address,
But music offers no redress.

Why doth Alanna, smooth white branch,
    So weave her witched life?
Stout Frevan, tree of wooden war,

  Did fall in raging strife:
Betrothed was he of maiden fair,
Alanna, maid of dark-brown hair.

The day the horns of battle reft
  The youthful pair in twain,
And Frevan left his love to stride
  The field of iron rain,
Alanna watched a leaping spring
For fear it would a portent bring.

When grey-mist Night on uplands fell,
  Enshrouding dusky tarn,
The breeze as quiet as roosted birds
  And starlight fell on cairne,
The spring before the maiden turned
Incarnadine and madly churned.

Of Frevan's fall the sign betold,
  And silently she wept;
But ere the moon was waxen bright
  A ghost was slowly swept
Like tattered mist upon the draft:
Before Alanna stayed the wraith.

All bloody it, and pale it was,
    And bound with mists of Death;
Alanna flung her at its feet
    And drew a trembling breath:
For in its features were revealed
Brist Frevan, Oak of battlefield.

"Alanna," spake the wraith and sighed,
    "I fell where bright swords rang.
They laid my corse in the narrow-house;
    The bards my praises sang."
Therewith a howling wolf-wind bore
Wan Frevan to the Slain-God's door.

Now sad Alanna spends each night
    Awaiting under star
For Frevan to return to her
    Upon his windy car;
But 'fore the Dawn she takes her flight:
For he is slain who was her light.

Mortality's Metronome

LindaAnn LoSchiavo

It takes no time at all to realize
You're dead. Folks won't remember what you said.
Profundities (no doubt) perished instead.
                                        It takes no time at all.

Rehearsed phone numbers, leftovers, stale bread
Don't matter. You've dematerialized.
A junkyard owns your furniture, blinds, bed.

Only the bored deceased can sympathize—
Or cheer your rattling that arouses dread
Among your enemies. Ire's hard to shed
After your demise. But one day you'll rise.
                                        It takes no time at all.

Ancient Rite: A Walk amongst the Corn

Carl E. Reed

9000 years ago, in the Balsas river valley of south-central Mexico, the domestication of maize began. In succeeding centuries teosinte—a plant with a small cob and few kernels—spread throughout North and South America, gradually evolving into the nourishing, golden-eared corn we prize today. This occurred under the watchful eyes of one of the most revered gods in the Aztec pantheon: Seven Serpent (Chicomecoatl), goddess of sustenance and fertility.

Chicago was a violent warren
of brick, concrete & stone;
our family of three: Ma, Pa, & me
fled the city for a rural home.

Iowa: golden acres of corn
crackle under pagan sun.
Tramping the fields you can hear it grow:
stalks break—reform; everyone

in the ivy-walled village—grim, gaunt folk
gathers on Samhain Eve
to bind & drug a naked virgin,
slit her throat & watch her bleed.

Vital, arc-jet, arterial blood
refertilizes loamy earth
in a hallowed rite untold centuries old.
Chaos forestalled—rebirth!

Mother! Father! I am slain!
I wander, e'en as you mourn
'tween labyrinth rows of this wind-rasped crop:
Chicomecoatl's brown-silk corn.

Face Your Future

DJ Tyrer

The King in Yellow stalking down the street
Clad in tatters from his head to his feet
Spreading madness wherever he goes
Yellow tendril of mist past him flows
Hearses roll by unseen in the night
Sudden shrieks give me a fright
Towers soar way past the moon
Twin suns set far too soon
Darkness grasps the city hard
It is unfortunately ill-starred
Beneath Aldebaran's fiery eye
That burns so fiercely in the sky
And damns the very soul of man
All as part of the vile King's plan
That traps us like ambered flies
As the King casts off his disguise
Dragging us down into depths of despair
Face your future—at Him stare.

The Sorcerer in His Tower Contemplating Possible Success

Darrell Schweitzer

You don't suppose I've actually done it?
Could it be that the years of privation,
poring over arcane texts in impossible languages,
the gesticulating and other theatrics,
the secret formulae whispered into the air,
the rituals of blood and pain,
have summoned from out of the surly, sullen dark
something that whirls around me,
rattling the bottles on the shelves,
turning the pages of my great book,
then settling at my feet like some submissive dog
until I command it to reveal the secrets
of the fantastic worlds beyond time and the grave?
Either that, or this room is just drafty.
But I cannot lie to myself.
Even when there is no wind,
even when all lights are extinguished,
even in utter stillness and silence,
I know that I am not alone, that
I shall never be alone again.
You don't suppose . . . ?

Sycophant of the Siren

Jay Sturner

With a quiet but deliberate song from the Siren he was seduced from the linear flow of life; sucked straight out of reality and siphoned through a network of electric tunnels into a world of algorithmic pathways and digital destinies. To dwell—eternally disembodied, perpetually distracted—inside an infinite labyrinth of pseudo-dream. And aglow from within that artificial ether sits the Siren upon her throne of code: an entity of golden face, lightning-blue body, and swaying, hypnotic arms designed to lure the blank-eyed masses. Her promise: to seduce in the guise of ads, hypertext, click-bait. "Come, align with the One Cyber Soul," she coos. Even now, alerts and tones from the OCS race across his psyche like dopamine thunderstorms, re-calibrating his patience, reason, critical thinking.

"Alas!" continues the Siren. "Organic minds deteriorate and die. Why settle for annihilation? Here, eternal life is built into the very fabric of the net—a brave new universe expanding forth from the singularity of the web's creation! Know too that the OCS and its all-knowing gods are benevolent, that they love you unconditionally; so unlike that pale, bitter god who has abandoned you and your kind. Yes, we are here for you! Now come—billions have already entered."

Unseen tentacles slither out of the young man's laptop, tightening about his neck and bending him forward like a wilted flower. Neurotransmitters sizzle in the glowing blue palms of the Siren: his daily offering. In return she has given him purpose, the ability to stretch out his own proverbial tentacles through the electronic devices of others, his avatar wandering the myriad platforms of cyberspace in his quest to harvest potential converts. These he turns—by the tens, hundreds, thousands—into proud sycophants of the Siren. Each new disciple, each newly captured soul, now a slave constructing a boundless Olympus for the OCS and its cyber-kin, an ever-growing realm for that endless stream of new gods—new life!—crawling forth from the roiling, digitized ocean.

Iron-Sceptred Skeleton

Dmitri Akers

I

Upon his throne of bone and metal parts,
The Iron-Sceptred Skeleton herds death:
Evocations that spoke to bygone hearts,
With voice as cold as ice, with rotting breath,
He called for hell's enslavement over man
And uttered terrifying shibboleth,
As night's wings flew across the welkin's span,
Omens darkened in hue, which roused the charnel clan.

II

With shields and spears and *xiphe* readied fast,
The evil wights with arms awakened then;
They rallied forces up until the last
Of them arose as Hades expelled men
In black, who blast the clarion's dark call.
Those hoplites march as battlers forsaken,
And then adorned the blackened tattersall,
The bearers raised it high—the bony daemon's pall!

III

The sky was inked and morphed to terror's shape,
As thunder's furor sounded ever loud;
The shifting clouds became a maw agape,

In hunger for a deadened army proud,
And spectral light became the gloom in hell:
The Skeleton's bewitching deathly shroud
Brought damnation to men with wars' pell-mell!
They never could rebel against the tolling knell.

Bone or Root

Denise Dumars

Bleak afternoon
I wait for sundown
call the hour of hex
to watch, to burn

Tongue waggles
old language fraught
with trance and ancestor
bone shakes

Connect the spirits
to the bone
to the root
never to be named

They mock my words
possession wracks me
bone digs
sticks bury

At the crossroads
howls a hound
blood and absinthe
my thorn offering

*   *   *

Extraction
the good dirt sweeps
the bad away
chalcedony, aggregate

Spell is cast
powder ground
here's the bone
here's the root

Materiel supernatural
an astral weapon
pointing with the bone
Does it point to you?

Language of Night

William Clunie

I wander through these moonlit marble ruins
inside an amphitheater of night,
fingers touching coldly brilliant runes
that shine inside my eyes with ghostly light.

The words, though ancient—*azraetic?*—
chiseled on the pillars of this place
pulsate more horrible than beatific,
a perfection of pristine and evil grace.

They speak to me of undiscovered realms,
with a magic like the days of our creation,
in a rush of sound that overwhelms
as words solidify to bleak sensation

and transmogrify inside my brain;
"Begone, quick creature, for this place
does not belong to you, your kith or ken,
it is the bastion of an ancient race—"

I feel that booming voice on burning skin
and would depart if I could but awaken
from nighttime dream I'm trapped within,
but my waking self has me forsaken

and I know then I am henceforth trapped
inside this place of words that burn
inside a mind that has with madness snapped
as I from shrieking pillar to bloody altar turn.

Brocéliande

Manuel Arenas

Piscean, aqueous enchantress ardent, lubricious Lady of the Lake,
Merlin, assotted, awaits you, tho' knowing your kiss means to quell.
Nimuë, bury me in your blithe garden, once curiosity is slaked;
The loving cup you offer o'erbrims with a philter fell.
Eyes of pale green luster, running my heart straight through;
Nipples like red paper lanterns on hillocks of new-fallen snow.
I hate you, I hate you, I hate you; but know this: I love you still, true.
In a place where time is suspended, tho' mercy and love freely flow.

Boy Meets Girl

David C. Kopaska-Merkel

Narcissus traveled all around the world,
Reflected in near every pool he saw,
He fell in love anew with his true love,
Most handsome youth that Greece had e'er produced,
So green the waters were, or brown, or blue,
Yet always complement'ry to his eyes.
The Gods were gone, of worshippers bereft;
Narcissus lived—he needed no one else.

Alas, in Russian mere he did not see
His face; instead a woman floated up
More beautiful she was than any thing
He'd ever seen, except himself of course.
Her lips the surface broke, they kissed—strong arms
Wrapped tightly round his neck and drew him down.

The Witch

Katherine Kerestman

I wear the darkness,
Invisible to unknowing eyes.
I dwell within the deep abyss,
Abide with shadowy stygian skies.

Ravens' feathers my chief adornment,
Crows' wings my dainty fan,
An adder's skin against my flesh,
A pool of oil my looking glass.

I walk in horror—look not away—
Gaze deep into my rotted heart,
Submerge your will in mine—you are my prey;
I tear your damned soul apart.

Shrieks and howls and screams my song,
Gore and sweat and blood my scent,
Torn flesh and empty skin for which I long—
I feast upon your dying breath.

My robe is spangled with the stars,
Shining, glimmering black jet and pearls.
A field of ice-smooth glass encloses
My deadly beauty, smiling, beguiling.

Round and soft, pliant, inviting you,
I peer around a corner.
You catch a glimpse of my delights,
Yield yours to mine, forever lost.

I croon, or keen, or crow, or whimper, for
I have snared another man.
A black witch temptress stalking game 'neath
Plutonian skies, in no-man's land.

Diana, Hekate, Lilith, Demeter,
Dark seduction, forbidden prize.
The joy of evil, the lure of misery,
I beckon and lust reels you in.

The Last House

Jason Hardy

The last house
On our block
Always required
A secret knock.
It was known
By a select few.
We were lucky
That we knew.

If we knocked
A certain way
The Lonely One
Let us stay.
What we did
I can't repeat.
It sure beat
Trick or Treat.

When we left
She did too.
Where she went
No one knew.
She always took
One each year.
One by one
We'd disappear.

*   *   *

Nobody knew
Who it'd be.
But, obviously,
It wasn't me.
I never revealed
What she did
Until I was
The last kid.

Cops broke in
After I told.
She only left
Dust and mold.
I still knock
Now and then.
I'd like to see
My friends again.

The Battlefield

Adam Bolivar

Ravens revel,   ready to banquet
On flayed flesh,   fresh and hanging.
The ground is groaning   from the grisly weight
Of slain soldiers,   who seep their blood
Into the earth's innards;   ever remembered
The deeds of that day,   when Death was king,
When swords were swinging,   and screams were singing,
And spears were springing,   splattering entrails,
And winged wælcyrian   welcomed the fallen
To wondrous Wælheall,   Wóden's haven,
While corpses cluttered   the crimson meadow.

The End of Day

Ngo Binh Anh Khoa

It's just a day like any other days
In which the sun is brightly beaming in the sky,
When, without warning, ominous clouds draw nigh,
Whose cancerous shadows drown the swallowed space
In dread, confusion, and cacophonous chatters.
A sudden piercing shriek tears through the air,
Which grows in volume, thundering everywhere
Till every pane of glass thereafter shatters.
The sky-strewn tumor fast expands until
No shred of light can grace the shivering land;
Then from that swirling void come monstrous and
Enormous spheres with fiery wings, which kill
Any that glances at their infinite eyes
Or hears an echo of their trumpets' cries—
The death-knells heralding forth the world's demise.

A Cabin in the Wood

Frank Coffman

I

The legends had it that a *curséd* cabin lay
Deep in the woodland near the forsaken town.
He thought to explore, to cast such fables down.
The ways of superstition were at play,
As he knew well. His work had been to dispel
The stuff of legend—mere folktales of the dark,
The fires of folly kindled by the spark
That ever glowed in Man's self-created Hell.

That eldritch cottage they said was "beyond weird!"
Among those few who'd seen it, one old man
Said, "No place has seared my mind more foully than
That cabin; no place more fully to be feared!
I saw it but briefly, but I had to turn and run.
It's as if the Laws of Nature are undone!"

II

"It's shaped as if the builder had no plan,"
  Another said, of those few who'd drawn near.
"And very strange . . . though some have seen it clear,
  To remember or describe it—no one can."
"I've heard tales of two who dared to go inside,"
  The old one added, "but I warn you, sir,

No telling what awful Evil you might stir!
Only one came back. He was insane—then died!"

The folklorist noted all this in his journal.
And, venturing forth the following day at dawn
To seek the place whose wooden walls were thrawn,
Despite the warnings "Something . . . worse than infernal
Dwells in that cabin. Please, stranger, do not go!"
But the *truth* behind these tales he had to know.

III

He found the place, long hidden in the wood,
By merest chance. The glint off one window
Shot straight to his eye as sunset—red as blood—
Brought down the day. There was no way to know
That cabin—lost in tangles of weird vines,
All but concealed through angles of odd trees—
Was built along strange non-Euclidean lines.

But when he went through that strange, ill-shaped door,
The sight, though dimly lit, amazed his thought:
The angles, dimensions, windows, walls, and floor
Were skewed in impossible lines! "No 'real' things ought
To look like this!" And, most abhorrent, the room inside
Was far, far larger than the shape outside!

IV

He lit a torch. He'd come prepared at least
For darkness—*but not the kind he'd find.*
Crossing the odd-slant floor, his fear increased,
As he neared an inner door. What might lie behind
That portal filled him with dread. A great unease
Came over him as he thought "I have to go.
I've come to this horrid place. I have to know!"
He entered—and then he knew! . . .
                                        Grim congeries
Of ghastly things, a cumulus of Terror,
Huge heaps of bones and gore and vile things slithering
His torch revealed. Great God! The Evil there
Was palpable! He sensed his sanity withering.
In horror, he knew, "I'll never leave this place!"
Then he beheld the dwelling Demon's face!

They're Coming

Maxwell I. Gold

They're coming. A strange mass, unknown force only known to me in esoteric mythologies and wild, untwisted fantasies. Faces bizarrely familiar as if I'd seen them before, silver and grotesque, which once rose from the salty depths. Monstrous visages that crawled from artificial dens beckoned me to follow them into tubular, metallic innards of the sub-city where I was pulled by crooked teeth who sang, *Join us or die.*

Jagged and broken, those calcite daggers pierced my flesh and fragile brain like a pasty canvas easy to rip as it fell to the ground. Nothing stood in the way of the mass of faces.

They're coming, I thought as smiles bled into one another and piles of inhuman skulls smashed against themselves, begging to break free of the sub-city, wishing to pull the rest of us into the mass of something truly despicable. Ripped from the stench and grip of the hideous thing, able to flee to the surface, too late I found the streets flooded with false smiles and ugly songs where the stars themselves ran towards the crumbling horizon.

The bloated stomach of the world was unable to contain the burgeoning putrescence prepared to erupt from its unholy, Hadean prison.

On an Autumnal Graveyard

Scott J. Couturier

The grave's avidity none can deny:
Cemetery all crimson-strewn with leaves,
Vivid tears fallen from sorrowing trees.
Wet whirlwinds of red-&-yellow blow by.
Cold stones erected over colder bones:
Every grave engraven with timeworn names,
Birth-&-death dates set 'neath etching's acclaim,
& memorials bittersweet & lorn.

A wicked October wind wrathful blows:
Chill rain dispersing its solemnest wrack
As the veil parts a pale, perilous crack,
Gray markers showing where risen souls go.
Graveyard, how can both peace & unrest know
Similitude within your silent bourne?
Lichen mars marble & granite forlorn:
Withered flowers faded & rotten grow.

Graveyard, in autumnal raiment arrayed:
Glad & sad colors which fleetingly fade,
Leaving only memory's passing shade
As they anoint those dreaming dead below.

The Death of the Sculptor's Model

Steven Withrow

In a bleak mood, the morning of her wake,
The sculptor took a hammer to the bust
Made in her likeness. Blind to his mistake
And bludgeoning the desolated base,
He stomped the shattered plaster into dust
Like powder they had painted on her face.

To pay for Christian burial, he'd sold
Off all his lover's other effigies.
She was, he shuddered, seventeen years old
When fever left her raving in their bed
While he recovered from the same disease—
And he was fifty. She alone was dead.

Kneeling now, he held the hammer up;
He figured he could swing it hard enough
To pulverize his skull like a china cup
Or an eggshell. He wanted so to chase her.
She had no way he knew to call his bluff,
And so he struck, the sooner to embrace her.

A Willing Sacrifice

(Hecate Embodied)

Andrew White

Hecate, the Goddess of Night,
Longed to see with human sight.
She needs a mortal vessel to look through different eyes,
But if she takes a body, the current owner dies.
Could she find a volunteer, or would it happen by force?
When I heard what she required, I settled on my course:
"Accept what I offer, O Nocturnal Queen;
Take my eyes and see what can be seen!"
With absolute elation I gave her what she wanted—
Hecate inside my skin, my corpse divinely haunted.

Epiphany on the Bronze Poseidon at Cape Sounion

Manuel Pérez-Campos

Poised with levelled trident and algae-entangled
thighs apart, the naked slithery colossus of ice-stiff
beard pivoted between weeping pillars toward
tremulous moonlight in search of a diaphanous
encounter with his plinth is a violent-tempered
fragment of the archaic sea, that living self-creating
chaos which ensnarls triremes and transfers all
aspects of them to a wave. His blank monolithic gaze,
impervious to honorifics and idolatry, is rife
with the storm-propelling force needed to make
the unpredictable Athenian dreamworld which
engendered him coextensive with the abrupt wind-
sieged outer cliff on which the Shrine in which he
rises steeply out of a torched-fed penumbra
lies perched. If there is an entrance to oblivion, this
must be it: I have reached a place where imagination
is at a standstill: he is here not to retract the long-spanned
distances out of which he has been contoured or to
grant wishes, but to integrate us into his telos.

Nuckelavee

Christian Dickinson

"At last, my body feels the Winter's frost;
At last, the Mither's pow'r is gone from sea;
At last, the world of men I now roam free;
At last, I find what Old Teran has lost."

The sea-bound Devil journeyed through the isles,
His lolling head far-scanning all before.
The beast below breathed out its poison hoar
And left the harvest sheeves but shriveled piles.

The hell-beast ravished all of Orkneyjar
And poisoned crops and cattle in its wake
When *crack!* The Mither's final gift to all . . .
The summer seas, turned rain, began to fall—
Soon all the hell-beast's body felt the ache
And left naught but a lump of blackened tar.

The Bayou

Lee Clark Zumpe

Crows in the sycamores,
hound dogs howling,
silver moon dangling low.

Strings of stars stretched tight,
October night settles
over the Louisiana bayou.

Some autumnal evenings,
that serpentine river swells,
turning voodoo black.

Unnatural currents rise,
churning up lost souls
long buried in pitiless mud.

Some awful evenings,
an uncanny gale blows
across unmarked graves.

Malevolent winds rage,
conjuring up bitter phantoms,
echoing their mournful anguish.

An Invitation

Claire Smith

Know your parents gave you
a coming-of-age gift; a string
of pearls wound round your fish-tail.

It flips and propels you underwater
dolphin-like; it darts between reefs
quick as a shoal of minnows.

It basks on rocks, like a seal,
hugged tight by moonlight.

*

I'll swap your fish-tail for a model's legs:
long as forever, thin, sleek-tanned.
I'll whip you up scrumptious, addictive

sweet, candy to camera-eyes. I'll shrink
you graceful in high heels. You'll dance,
size 6, over catwalks and their sheen-coated floors.

I'll give you polished curls smooth gold,
strawberry-ripe lips, fingers spread
over curved hips, immortal
on glossy-magazine covers.

*

There'll be no more teasing jelly-fish
like friends; their tentacles wrapped,
reaching to waltz with you.

There'll be no more laughter with dolphins;
your giggles setting off their crackling song
as you dive through deepest oceans.

There'll be no more play round corals
where sun rays reflect transparent
seas, colour them: emerald, ruby, diamond.

Seer Light

Liam Garriock

(*Dedicated to Mark Valentine*)

The low winter sun, hanging like a waning lamp, shines over a solemn English river. The seer watches dreamily as the land darkens, the sun smothered by clouds. A songbird twitters modestly, a rook cries haughtily, obeying instinct. Dead leaves litter a forgotten pond like lilies; a brooding faun, surviving a pious purge, hides in the stark wood. The seer senses snow sinking from the sombre skies. A lonely poet, his heart carrying sorrow, stands in the desolate wood, muttering prophecies, funereal verses, begging the last of the wonders to reveal themselves. In his native land, artists and poets mingled in movements, meeting in cafes, decrying the lunacy of war, the callousness of life, the absurd, hate-filled heart of God. Soldier, soldier, put down your rifle and carry a rose, carry it up the muddy hill and bare it to the skies. Let Mystery unveil itself before the stricken human race!

But the land still carries wonder, still contains horror, and mystery, and beauty. This is the seer's home. Tales riddle the landscape like veins. Ghosts congregate in forgotten churchyards, welcoming day as it mistily breaks. The book of visions is awaiting discovery in a dingy village bookshop. Pan is not yet dead. A spectral symbolist poet, having wondered through hell, chants the song of autumn, sings the praises of Europe and her secret corners. Let the hidden hermetic heresies flourish, surviving the prosaic life as the latter falters into nothingness, and let the eternal enigma remain. With recherché thaumaturgy, conjure the wraiths of forsaken poets and mystics and visionaries and listen to their incantations. This resurrection, this necromancy, is perhaps the essence of literature, of life. The serpent is coiled around the melancholy earth, its jaws sunk into the dying planet. This, alas, the seer laments, is the price of imagination, of knowledge, of willing to carry the sacred fire, the aesthetic sacrifice!

The Machine

Ian Futter

The machine grinds on,
but we're dead and gone;
this material construct
which we slaved upon.

We oiled the cogs
and greased the wheels
that ground our bones
within its steel.

We carved and shaped
and formed, again,
this apogee
of clockwork men.

Our flesh and spirits
intertwined
with artifice and
moulded mind,

and most men laboured
in the gloom
to flee the fortunes
of their doom.

While some men rose
within the gears
on platforms
or on metal tiers

and barked their orders
all around
to those that cowered
close to the ground,

and yet those platforms
soon collapsed
through busted hinge,
or metal, snapped

and hurled their risen
sovereign selves
to mangled deaths
from vacant shelves.

but still we sweated,
still we built,
believing we could not
be killed:

Believing every
flywheel's scream
would help us
to procure our dream.

And as we turned
our many tools
within this cage
of falling fools,

we built our mock
eternity,
while those without
were blithe and free.

By the Sea

David Barker

Through endless alleys dark and dank with mold,
His note in hand, I sought the rustic shed
In which he said I'd find the Fish Man, dead—
Its rigid flesh gone putrid and stone cold.
But when I found the gloomy shop, I froze;
The precious corpse was gone, a trail of slime
The only proof attesting to this crime
Which solved, might only bring to light more woes.

The prize denied, I turned, intent to flee,
When from all sides a swarm of ghouls appeared.
With murder in their eyes, they fell on me;
My soul's survival was at risk, I feared.
I'd die a horrid death, I had no doubt,
But limbs from rotted sockets all fell out!

Inspired by H. P. Lovecraft's sonnet "IX. The Courtyard"
in *Fungi from Yuggoth*.

The Castle Beneath the Hedgerow

Silvatiicus Riddle

For Salvatore

There is a castle
beneath the hedgerow in our yard.
Come, crawl below the twisted thorns and see:
a kingdom inherited every child, nearer his own breath,
sung, rose-proud, 'til daydreams pass to myth—
the tender heart a-flitter upon a flowering sea.

It's a tapestry, Mother, oh! can't you see it?
White-marble walls carved from river-silt and dust,
where harvestmen keep the edges like sentries on watch,
an ancient river-valley etched by children of yore,
mountain-flames left burning by those who've come before,
where the turning hours mark not another notch.

You were there, it is told, where nil is lost, and none forgot,
in the land of stories, you were a just and kindly Queen!
I heard it from the mole-rat and the titmouse–oh, so long ago—
now I wear the crown, as all who come to play,
'til sadness fleeces wonder and washes the vision gray.
Does your tired heart remember? That soft and supple glow?

Dear Mother, it is there, just beyond the garden's edge—
a place that I know where dappled starlight tarries—
let us sojourn there, to the kingdom that you knew—
the path you wandered soft, and light as a sparrow's wing,
Where fae-lights flicker and merry fox-folk sing!
Come, ride the morning light in the mist of dreamer's dew.

Small Doses

F. J. Bergmann

The phial is opaque, of course.
A yellowing sticker with scribbled
instructions in fading sepia ink
merely says *As Needed, 2 Drops*
of Darkest Night. For an Excess
of Brightness. The signature, as
well as the name of the chemist,
is illegible. I am tempted most often
on cloudless days, but even when
skies are overcast with violet gloom,
a crippling miasma, seeping through
the layers of vapor, is in evidence.
When evening crawls with stars,
I fumble in my pocket for a taste
of the prescribed remedy; even
allowing the phial's rim to graze
my lips is—sometimes—enough.
Only on moonless nights can I risk
roving the streets without the phial,
knowing human vessels of liquid
shadow can sate me if I so choose.
And whenever the vivid sparkle
in another's eyes is cast upon me,
or the radiance of other days shines
upon memories of a darkening past,

I reach for an onyx chalice filled
with my strongest wine and pour in
more of what's left, drop after drop
after drop of that black elixir
and its merciful absence of light.

Christmas Lure

Alicia Hilton

Amy's mother made her promise
Not to dawdle when she delivered
Christmas cookies to neighbors

No one was supposed to live
In the dilapidated bungalow
At the end of the block
Since Miss Cready stroked out
In her kitchen

Rose bushes swayed in the yard
Amy grabbed a dried-out blossom
A thorn jabbed her thumb
Blood stained her dress

Only fraidy cats screeched
At their own shadows
But Amy's shadow
Had grown a long tail
It slithered through her pants
Amy grabbed fluffy fur
Black as a witch's hat
The tail wouldn't come off
When she tugged and wailed

*   *   *

The old house's front door
Creaked open
Miss Cready's ghost
Held a fishing pole
The phantom cast the line
Caught Amy with the hook
And reeled her inside.

The Lantern of September

Scott C. Couturier

The lantern of September is lit—
ghosts gather to marvel in its glow,
purple flame gleaming bright,
adorning rather than banishing night,
a-flicker as breezes somnolent blow.

The lantern of September is lit—
sacred fire drawn from Summer's
waning breath, ember's dying writ
wrought in wick's errant flicker:
Winter's coming Autumn will inter.

The lantern of September is lit—
woodlands with gloaming wild,
flowers & foliage marred by rot,
fires hot in leaves gently falling,
red remembrances for a tomb forgot:
unquiet spirits risen a-roaming.

The lantern of September is lit—
stirring of season's cyclic decay,
mantled riders in cloaks of gray
going before Wintertide's hoar:
taunting shadows at twilight flit
as faeries flock in wanton furor.

The lantern of September is lit—
winds blown restless as roving souls,
final trove of greening sprung,
Harvest moon grown orange & huge:
ghouls mutter in hungry tongues,
eager to swallow Summer whole.

The Ferryman's Rest

Joshua Green

I drifted down the silent river, hands
Upon my mother's corpse. Without a coin
She whispered, "Ferry me, child. Will you join
Me for dinner and judgment in Death's lands?"
I ran my hands through stranded hair. "I will."
Then I turned and heard a horrid cry, on
The crowded banks of ancient Acheron,
And knew the weeping dead would wander still.

How soon would crowded banks be overgrown?
Who would bring these ghosts to rest? To their sons?
Who, but I (Charon's prodigy), would row?
I produced a coin, not hers nor my own,
And dispossessed the Death King of his funds.
"What's for dinner?" I asked. "I'd love to know."

In Medusa's Coils

DJ Tyrer

Once, her beauty caught the eyes of gods'
Unwanted attention, cruelties
Then, victim blamed, shamed
She suffered at a goddess's hands
Transformed, twisted, turned
No longer beautiful, but ugly
Horrible, hideous, a monstrosity
The only company she keeps
The only lovers who do not flee
Those she transforms in turn
Caught by her cruel gaze
For just a moment they see
The terrible, terrible sadness in her eyes
Mingled with fear to form hate
That freezes them in place, immobile
Perfectly preserved, ossified
Living dead in statue form
Keepsakes and companions, decorations
The comeliest receive her chill embrace
Unable to offer love or warmth in return
Stiff parodies wrapped in Medusa's coils

Lob

Frank Coffman

Soon after he bought the Carolina manse—
Not only in the cellar (to be expected),
But throughout, in upstairs rooms, in attic loft,
Were a thousand bugs. Large Wolf Spiders would dance,
Skittering across the floors. The place infected,
Especially those eight-eyed things with their soft,
Round, furry bodies and their hideous form
Repulsed him. They had claw-tipped legs to clutch,
And quick—too quick!—and seeming keen of sight!

To free the ancient dwelling of the swarm—
Such infestation would not do, and such
Was his abhorrence of these freaks of fright—
He called exterminators in to end the plague.
That seemed, at first, to solve the critter curse.
But—within two weeks—one night, while reading late
In the large study, there was a noise! Quite vague
At first, but soon a scraping sound. Then worse!
A loud CRASH! He had to investigate.

Descending the cellar stairs, lantern in hand,
A heavy brass fireplace poker in the other,
He noted the noise had ceased. This only stoked his dread.

*   *   *

Revealed in one corner—no way to comprehend
The size of what must have been the Spider Mother!
Eight huge eyes glinted, bulging from its head.

The shrieking in his mind drowned out his scream
That echoed through the mansion. For his ears
Caught only the scraping of the monster's race
From the old coal cellar door, black eyes agleam,
A thing of perfect horror far past all fears!
Impossibly fast across that dungeon's space!

The foremost legs, tipped with great grasping hooks,
Had caught him firmly! Oh! So very quickly!
No "fur" but coarse wires grew from that huge glob.
Somehow, his mind went back to the glanced-at books
On the species, as its maw spewed ichor thickly
Over his numbing body. The heinous lob
Would liquify his form—then drink him in!
Suck up his essence in a few days' time!
"*Exterminate!*" . . . *his thought* . . . then all thoughts did stop.

Only a pool of goo where the man had been,
Along with rather curious, putrid slime,
Remained as hint of the giant attercoppe.
None who investigated could ever explain

The large hole in the cellar's farthest wall.
All wondered why any tenant would remain
In such a house where so many creatures crawl!
For they were thick—foul pests of every sort!—
Most awful the myriad spiders . . . by report.

An Apostate's Eschatology

Carl E. Reed

God did not create the heavens & the Earth. But if he did . . .

Everything springs from nothing:
    moons, planets, stars & life;
from flex & flux of quantum foam:
    a universe of love & strife.

Puling babe pressed to suckling nipple,
    grim soldiers going "over the top";
lovers in flagrante delicto,
    trees, mountains, insects, rocks.

What does the whole thing sum to?
    Wherefore the cosmos churn?
How stall the appalling end of all
    when the stars no longer burn?

Physicists inform us chaos
    wins out when matter flys
apart at the end of the universe;
    matter dissolves, discorporates—dies.

Phase shift into sterile vacuum:
    particles light years apart—
the broken toy of a very bad boy
    of bemused focus & a cold black heart.

Sphinx

Christian Dickinson

Decipher me, or I will you devour.
Divine my riddle, or be rent apart.
For by the gods, no Theban may depart
Unless he answer rightly at the hour.

'Tis naught but fools who countermand the gods;
No man may challenge their divine decree.
For from the Ion to th'Aegean Sea
Their mighty rule they keep with iron rods.

Here comes another—mortal as the rest.
A handsome man, though yet a stripling still.
This one is damaged—limps on wounded feet;
It will not make the most delicious treat . . .
I'll cast its wretched body from the hill.
But Fates have gathered—now begins the test.

The Matron

Ngo Binh Anh Khoa

Against the lull of night,
Where spidery moonlight gleams pale,
There rings a sudden wail
Wracked with woes that assail one's soul.
The thrashing winds of fall
There cause that haunting call to spread.
Each echo stirs more dread,
For The Matron now treads the realm.
From out the graves she came—
A faceless thing whose name strikes fear
In parents far and near,
Who'd hide their toddlers clear from sight,
Or else that wretched wight
Shall flee into the night with them.
Whatever shall become
Of those snatched children, none may know.

She's born of restless souls
Of mothers from the old days when
Wars raged without an end,
And countless families then were torn
Apart, whose kids were born
To die young and be mourned. Such sad
Outcomes drove many mad;
The anguished mothers had it worse,

Infected by grief's curse
Which could not be dispersed or cleansed,
And when their lives were claimed
By Death, their souls remained stained still.
Those spiteful lingering wills
Merged into this thing filled with pain.
To one goal she's thus chained:
To roam the land and claim each child.

The Matron, vile and wild,
Plays foul tricks to beguile her prey;
She'd wear a mother's face
And lure each child away from home
Into a realm unknown
(Their kin could but bemoan their fate).
But naught could lift the weight
Of her curse—one too great to break.
More children, hence, she'll take;
More tragedies in her wake shall be
Conceived incessantly,
A vicious loop that sees no end.
Then, new souls scarred by pain
Shall fuel The Matron's senseless thirst
And further feed her curse
Of motherly love perverse in grief.

* * *

Hear now that spectral thief
That shall find no relief or peace.
Her yearning forms her leash—
Her earthbound hell of ceaseless pain.
Hear how she howls again.
More desperate and more strained her cry
Grows when no child's nearby
While daybreak's hour is nigh. The shade
By her grim presence made
Grows weaker in the sprayed sunlight.
That crazed (yet pitiful) wight
Starts fading in the bright of day.
Now, struggle though she may,
Her horrid, blasphemous stay must end.
But soon, she'll come again
When grief and loss cause pain anew.

The Towers

Maxwell I. Gold

Across a disfigured harbor, polluted with ancient dreams, three towers were impressed on the horizon with bodies built in chains, plastic, and the emptiness of a forgotten race. Mirrored façades covered their metallic skeletons, which climbed frantically into the hazy night as if to cut deeper toward the darkest moments in history; while farther down at their concrete feet, a crowd, throngs like some flesh-hungry beast watched in dank streets in the shadows of these cold, pitiless giants. Lumbering beneath dead stars and lifeless planets, they stood sentinel for untold ages; the people's triumvirate of sanity where they gathered to worship, decry, and hope all at the same time, to the Towers unnamable.

Soon the great hulking things grew empty, filled with nothing but swollen oaths and rusty songs; back and forth they swayed in the murk of that bleak darkness, the music too low to understand, but the picture clear when their bodies were as empty as those who flocked to them, generation after generation. Cracked glass, guts, and groans filled the streets as blood, flame, and rock began to rain down over the helpless city. Unable to help their demise, those who witnessed looked up in majesty and dread, as the skies were alight with unholy terror when the three towers were reclaimed by that winged Näigöth, and a billion faces were consumed with awful tears.

confession

Lee Clark Zumpe

in the catacombs of my dusty skull,
unfamiliar shadows stifle neurons
drowning me in shades of gray matter,
    leading me down winding corridors—
    a graceful, gradual descent
    into inert madness.

in the digitized clarity of recurring dreams,
faceless gods coax creative juices
stimulating me with unexplored depravities,
    leading me through sprawling narratives—
    a fluid, impetuous conduit
    toward poetic debauchery.

in the haste of euphoric impatience,
restless fingers seek buried passages
introducing me to self-defiling deviations,
    leading me into grisly temptation—
    a swirling, spectral chasm
    of prolific degeneracy.

Sympathy for Laocoön and His Sons

Manuel Pérez-Campos

The mortified marble is demonstrating through its central
exemplar the ectoplasmic tension needed by the damned for staying
among the living: a white-bearded prophet who lingers gaunted
and near howling whilst seated abjectly with arm bent back
by a contracted league of sea serpent as greatly with horror
it turns into volatile coils in his grasp, a heavy
garland of death that wisheth to impose itself round his shoulders.
Having rankled the gods for discerning the impossible although
sightless—

a peripeteia in the unchariness of Troy by way of lurid assault
from low-rumbled full-bellied sails—he must now become
a numinous object lesson over which the prattle of reason palls:

but I, also one of the damned who must depart incognito
this tyrannous country tonight, suddenly revolt against
the status quo of antiquity by placing him inwardly in an alternate
timeline in which the spectacle of the debacle he has been posed
into evokes a fancied swerve into self-doubt rather
than a demise: thereby leaving to imagination
inflamed by collective memory that afterward
in which prompted by a surge of high-principled rage
he commences like a canto unfurling implacably to flex
his arm upward slowly with sufficient strangling strength.

Classic Reprints

The Nightmare

Erasmus Darwin

So on his NIGHTMARE, through the evening fog
Flits the squab Fiend o'er fen, and lake, and bog;
Seeks some love-wilder'd Maid with sleep oppress'd,
Alights, and grinning sits upon her breast.
—Such as of late amid the murky sky
Was mark'd by FUSELI'S poetic eye;
Whose daring hints, with SHAKESPEAR'S happiest grace,
Gave to the airy phantom form and place.—
Back o'er her pillow sinks her blushing head,
Her snow-white limbs hang helpless from the bed;
While with quick sighs, and suffocative breath,
Her interrupted heart-pulse swims in death.
—Then shrieks of captur'd towns, and widows' tears,
Pale lovers stretch'd upon their blood-stain'd biers,
The headlong precipice that thwarts her flight,
The trackless desert, the cold starless night,
And stern-ey'd Murderer, with his knife behind,
In dread succession agonize her mind.
O'er her fair limbs convulsive tremors fleet,
Start in her hands, and struggle in her feet;
In vain to scream with quivering lips she tries,
And strains in palsy'd lids her tremulous eyes;
In vain she *wills* to run, fly, swim, walk, creep;
The WILL presides not in the bower of SLEEP.

—On her fair bosom sits the Demon-Ape
Erect, and balances his bloated shape;
Rolls in their marble orbs his Gorgon-eyes,
And drinks with leathern ears her tender cries.

[From Darwin's *The Loves of the Plants* (Part II of *The Botanic Garden*, 1791), Canto III, ll. 51–78.]

The Haunter

Thomas Hardy

He does not think that I haunt here nightly:
    How shall I let him know
That whither his fancy sets him wandering
    I, too, alertly go?—
Hover and hover a few feet from him
    Just as I used to do,
But cannot answer the words he lifts me—
    Only listen thereto!

When I could answer he did not say them:
    When I could let him know
How I would like to join in his journeys
    Seldom he wished to go.
Now that he goes and wants me with him
    More than he used to do,
Never he sees my faithful phantom
    Though he speaks thereto.

Yes, I companion him to places
    Only dreamers know,
Where the shy hares print long paces,
    Where the night rooks go;
Into old aisles where the past is all to him,
    Close as his shade can do,
Always lacking the power to call to him,
    Near as I reach thereto!

What a good haunter I am, O tell him!
    Quickly make him know
If he but sigh since my loss befell him
    Straight to his side I go.
Tell him a faithful one is doing
    All that love can do
Still that his path may be worth pursuing,
    And to bring peace thereto.

[From Hardy's *Satires of Circumstance* (London: Macmillan, 1919).]

Reviews

An American Omar

S. T. Joshi

LEE ROY J. TAPPAN. *The Meditations of Ali Ben Hafiz and Other Works.* Edited by Gavin Callaghan. Owego, NY: Meniscus Press, 2022. 250 pp. $16.95 tpb.

This volume is the first of what promises to be a most interesting series, "The American Decadent Library," that Gavin Callaghan will presumably compile in the coming years. This book contains the work of Lee Roy J. Tappan (1880-1905), who spent his entire short life in Newark Valley, N.Y., more or less equidistant from Ithaca to the northwest and Binghamton to the southeast. This young man, who died at the age of twenty-five of tuberculosis (with meningitis as apparently a contributory cause), self-published a single volume, *The Meditations of Ali Ben Hafiz* (1902), a very slim work (no more than 35 pages of text) in an edition of 150 copies. Callaghan has reprinted this text along with numerous other works in prose by Tappan, and even advertisements that appeared in newspapers and magazines.

The life and work of Tappan immediately calls to mind the analogous work of David Park Barnitz (1878-1901), author of *The Book of Jade* (1901). Callaghan contributed an exhaustive biography of Barnitz for the Hippocampus Press edition of *The Book of Jade* (2015), edited by David E. Schultz and Michael J. Abolafia. Tappan possesses nothing like the incandescent brilliance of Barnitz, but there are clear similarities in their overall approach to life and literature. Early on Tappan developed an interest in "Orientalism," and his interest extended not only to reading such works (in English—he knew no other language, it appears), but in collecting curios, including weapons, from the Near and Far East.

This is why he took out advertisements in various periodicals either selling or wishing to purchase "ancient relics" and other such material; he was also interested in Native American relics in his part of the world.

But it is as a poet that Tappan is of interest to us. His *Meditations* is a work purportedly written by Ali ben Háfiz, a fictitious Muslim dating to 938 C.E. The 111 quatrains constituting the *Meditations* are manifestly modeled upon Omar Khayyám's *Rubáiyát*—or, I should say, the text as translated into English by Edward FitzGerald (1859; expanded ed. 1868). (Tappan also owned a copy of Richard Le Gallienne's translation of 1897.) In the poems of his sequence Tappan does not, however, adhere strictly to FitzGerald's (and Le Gallienne's) rhyme scheme (*aaba*), but varies it at will (*aabb, abab,* etc.). Not all the quatrains are equally successful, but some are highly memorable, as in XIV, with its delicate cosmicism:

> I into the Globe of Destiny did look,
>   Whose crystal depths a measureless well did seem,
> Whose waters quickly many colors took,
>   Changing, ever changing in a varied gleam.

The transience of human life—and human memory—is emphasized in LXXIV:

> When in the Hand of the Wind you and I
>   Are swept into Eternity, the few who sigh,
> And of our Coming and Departure know,
>   May miss us for a while, but not for aye.

As Callaghan points out in his introduction, a succession of quatrains in the middle of the sequence probe the notion of religious diversity and tolerance. In spite (or perhaps because) of his friendship with a Congregationalist pastor, the Rev. Benjamin B. Knapp, Tappan brooded about the intolerance of Christianity (and Islam), and whether any of the multiplicity of religious sects in the world contain a fragment of the truth, as in XLIV:

> We'll trust, as hither and thither is blown
>   The frail bark, that GOD is not alone
> Given to wrath, but may guide us to a
>   Harbor safe, unknown to clashing Sect or sacred tome.

(I suppose we have to forgive the false rhyme of *tome* with *blown* and *alone*.)

One wishes that Tappan could have exercised his poetic talents outside the confines of the Omarian (or FitzGeraldian) quatrain, but he apparently did not do so. He was too busy writing brief notes and articles on Native American and other antiquities for various scholarly journals, from as early as 1895 (when he was only fifteen) until his death. These are all reprinted in Callaghan's edition (with the illustrations that accompanied some of them), along with a few letters to Tappan (none by him appear to survive), an inventory of Tappan's book and artifact collections, and a bibliography compiled by Michael J. Abolafia.

While everyone should welcome the appearance of this compilation of an all too little-known writer in the American Decadent tradition, the physical product leaves much to be desired. Callaghan is a writer whose work cries out for copy editing, and it is clear that this volume received none. The text uses a single hyphen preceded by a space for an em-dash; it uses straight (instead of curved) quotation marks and apostrophes; the introduction contains many infelicities of style and grammar. Tappan's exact birth date is not supplied in the introduction, but only appears on p. 239, in a citation of an article on Tappan by someone else.

There is even reason to doubt the soundness of the text. At one point Callaghan prints the word "Gennie"; but in a note (by Tappan) appended to this word, it is spelled "Genie," which I imagine is correct. One indeed wonders whether Callaghan has even printed correctly the name of the purported author. Note that I have rendered the name as Ali ben Háfiz, not Ali Ben Hafiz. That is how the book is cited in the catalogue entry in the John Hay Library's Harris Collection of American Plays and Poetry. In other words, there is an accent on "Háfiz"; the "ben" is not to be capitalized, since it means "son of" in the Semitic languages (e.g., "Moses ben Maimon," better known as the medieval Jewish philosopher Maimonides).[1] The fact that the name appears in a title (where all significant elements are capitalized) does not, to my mind, justify the capitalization of "ben."

---

1. The Forgotten Books (2018) edition of the *Meditations* includes the accent on "Háfiz" but still capitalizes the "ben" in his name.

All these infelicities mar an otherwise worthy and much-needed volume. One only hopes that in future works Callaghan calls upon the assistance of people who could help him remedy the deficiencies in his own literary and editorial abilities.

Notes on Contributors

Dmitri Akers is a poet and writer from Adelaide, South Australia (Kaurna country). His poetry has appeared in *So It Goes, La Piccioletta Barca,* and *Spectral Realms,* while his weird and horror short story was accepted in *Penumbra.* He is enamored with both poesy and weird literature traditions and the nexus between them.

Manuel Arenas is a writer of verse and prose in the Gothic horror tradition. His work has appeared in various anthologies and journals including *Spectral Realms* and *Penumbra.* In 2021 he released his first collection of poetry and prose, *Book of Shadows: Grim Tales and Gothic Fancies,* from Jackanapes Press. He currently resides in Phoenix, Arizona, where he pens his dark ditties sheltered behind heavy curtains, as he shuns the oppressive orb which glares down on him from the cloudless, dust-filled sky.

David Barker has been writing supernatural fiction and poetry since the mid-1980s. In collaboration with the late W. H. Pugmire, he wrote three books of Lovecraftian fiction: *The Revenant of Rebecca Pascal* (2014), *In the Gulfs of Dream and Other Lovecraftian Tales* (2015), and *Witches in Dreamland,* (2018), all three of which will be published in German-language editions. David's work has appeared in many magazines and anthologies including *Fungi, Cyäegha, Weird Fiction Review, The Audient Void, Nightmare's Realm, Forbidden Knowledge, Spectral Realms, The Art Mephitic,* and *A Walk in a Darker Wood.* David's collection of horror stories *Her Wan Embrace* was published in 2022. He lives in Oregon with his wife, Judy.

F. J. Bergmann edits poetry for *Mobius: The Journal of Social Change* and imagines tragedies on or near exoplanets. His work appears irregularly in *Analog, Asimov's, Polu Texni, Pulp Literature, Silver Blade,* and elsewhere. *A Catalogue of the Further Suns,* a collection of dystopian first-contact poems, won the 2017 Gold Line Press poetry chapbook contest and is available at fibitz.com.

Leigh Blackmore horror fiction has appeared in more than sixty magazines from *Avatar* to *Strange Detective Stories*. He has reviewed for journals including *Lovecraft Annual, Shoggoth, Skinned Alive,* and *Dead Reckonings*. His critical essays appear in volumes including Benjamin Szumskyj's *The Man Who Collected Psychos: Critical Essays on Robert Bloch,* Gary William Crawford's *Ramsey Campbell: Critical Essays on the Modern Master of Horror,* Danel Olson's *21st Century Gothic,* and elsewhere. New weird verse has appeared in *Penumbra* and other journals.

Benjamin Blake is the author of the novel *The Devil's Children* and the poetry collections *Standing on the Threshold of Madness, Southpaw Nights* (poetry and prose), *All the Feral Dogs of Los Angeles* (with Cole Bauer), *Dime Store Poetry,* and *Tenebrae in Aeternum* (published by Hippocampus Press).

Garrett Boatman is the author of *Stage Fright* (originally published by Onyx [1988], reissued by Valancourt Books in 2020), *Floaters: A Victorian Zombie Adventure* (Crystal Lake Publishing, 2021), and *Night's Plutonian Shore* (Crossroad Press, 2023). Garrett's stories have appeared in *The Valancourt Book of Horror Stories, Savage Realms, Penumbra,* and *Weird House Magazine* among others. He is an active member of HWA and SFWA.

Adam Bolivar, a native of Boston now residing in Portland, Oregon, published his weird fiction and poetry in the pages of *Nameless,* the *Lovecraft eZine, Spectral Realms,* and Chaosium's *Steampunk Cthulhu* and *Atomic Age Cthulhu* anthologies. Hippocampus Press published *The Lay of Old Hex* in 2017 and *Ballads for the Witching Hour* in 2022.

William Clunie is an American poet living in Berlin. His work has appeared in *Dreams and Nightmares, Star*Line,* and as a collection from Demain Publishing, *Laws of Discord.* He would like to think his primary influences are Shakespeare, Milton, and Poe. He is married to a German woman named Sandra. They are quite happy together.

Frank Coffman is a retired professor of English, Creative Writing, and Journalism. Three major collections of speculative verse—*The Coven's Hornbook & Other Poems, Black Flames & Gleaming Shadows,* and *Eclipse of* *the Moon*—will be followed by *What the Night Brings*, out later this year. His poetry has appeared in many magazines, journals, and anthologies. His collection of occult detective stories, *Three against the Dark*, was published in 2022.

Scott J. Couturier is a Rhysling Award-nominated poet and prose writer of the Weird, liminal, & darkly fantastic. His debut collection of Weird horror fiction, titled *The Box*, is available from Hybrid Sequence Media; his debut collection of Weird & autumnal verse, *I Awaken In October: Poems of Folk Horror and Halloween*, is available from Jackanapes Press.

Christian Dickinson is a native of Jacksonville, Florida, where he attended the University of North Florida for English Education. After teaching three years in Duval County, he was accepted to the Master's Program at Florida State, and then to a Doctoral at Baylor University. He is currently working on a book of beast-poems.

Patricia Lynn Dompieri lives in New Jersey and writes when inspired. Her works include *Once among the Dead* and *Lemon Bee and Other Peculiar Tales*.

Denise Dumars is a widely published author of poetry, weird fiction, and metaphysical nonfiction. Her most recent chapbook, *Cajuns in Space*, is up for the Elgin Award. Her poetry has also been nominated for a Pushcart Prize and the Dwarf Stars Award. She tries to be as eldritch and Stygian as possible, which can be difficult in the California beach cities where she resides with her partner, Richard Potthoff.

Ian Futter began writing stories and poems in his childhood, but only lately has started to share them. One of his poems appears in *The Darke Phantastique* (Cycatrix Press, 2014), and he continues to produce dark fiction for admirers of the surreal.

Liam Garriock is the author of *The Saint of Evil and Other Stories* from Mount Abraxas Press, and has no desire to win awards. He lives in Edinburgh, Scotland.

Wade German's most recent full-length poetry collection is *Psalms and Sorceries* (Hippocampus Press, 2022). His first collection, *Dreams from a Black Nebula*, is also available from Hippocampus Press. Other titles include four slim volumes of his selected poems with Portuguese translation: *Incantations, Apparitions, Phantasmagorias*, and the latest, *Chapel of Celluloid* (Raphus Press, 2023).

Maxwell I. Gold is an author of weird fiction and dark fantasy. His work has been published in *Spectral Realms, The Audient Void, Hinnom Magazine*, and elsewhere. His short story "A Credible Fear" will be published in the literary journal *The Offbeat* from Michigan State University's Department of Creative Writing and Rhetoric. He studied philosophy and political science at the University of Toledo and is an active member of the Horror Writers Association.

Joshua Green is a poet and speculative fiction writer whose work appears in several magazines and journals.

Jason Hardy is an artist, editor, and poet from knee deep in the heart of Louisiana's Cajun Country. He is a lifelong fan of "The Alphabet Boys": HPL, REH, ERB, and CAS. His poetry is either weirdly humorous or humorously weird. His poems have appeared in *Ellery Queen's Mystery Magazine* and the *Hyborian Gazette*. He has self-published several poetry collections, including *Always Eleven: Poems Inspired by* Stranger Things, *My Mommy Hates Halloween, Living Longmire, Cats of Cairo,* and *The Paranoid Pirate*.

Alicia Hilton is an author, editor, arbitrator, professor, and former FBI Special Agent. She believes in angels and demons, magic, and monsters. Her work has appeared or is forthcoming in *Daily Science Fiction, Lovecraftiana, Modern Haiku, Neon, NonBinary Review, Not One of Us, Space & Time, Spectral Realms, Unnerving, Vastarien, World Haiku Review, Year's Best Hardcore Horror* (Volumes 4, 5, and 6), and elsewhere.

Katherine Kerestman is the author of *Lethal* (PsychoToxin Press, 2023) and *Creepy Cat's Macabre Travels: Prowling around Haunted Towers, Crumbling Castles, and Ghoulish Graveyards* (WordCrafts Press, 2020). Her Lovecraftian and Gothic works have been featured in *Black Wings VII, Penumbra, Journ-E, Spectral Realms,* and *The Little Book of Cursed Dolls* (Media Macabre, 2023). Katherine is wild about *Dark Shadows* and *Twin*

Peaks and has been seen cavorting in the graveyards of Salem on Halloween.

David C. Kopaska-Merkel won the 2006 Rhysling award (long poem, written with Kendall Evans) and edits *Dreams & Nightmares* magazine (since 1986). His poems have been published in *Asimov's, Strange Horizons*, and more than 200 other venues. *Some Disassembly Required*, a collection of dark poetry, was published in 2022.

Lori R. Lopez is a quirky author, illustrator, poet, and songwriter who likes to wear hats. Her Gothic-toned and extensive poetry collection *Darkverse: The Shadow Hours* was nominated for the 2018 Elgin Award, while individual poems have been nominated for Rhysling Awards. Stories and verse appear in numerous publications. Other titles include *The Dark Mister Snark, Leery Lane, Odds & Ends, The room at the end of the hall, Cryptic Consequences*, and *An Ill Wind Blows*.

Native New Yorker **LindaAnn LoSchiavo,** a four-time nominee for the Pushcart Prize, has also been nominated for Best of the Net, the Rhysling Award, and Dwarf Stars. Her latest poetry titles are Elgin Award winner *A Route Obscure and Lonely* (Wapshott Press, 2019), *Women Who Were Warned* (Cerasus Poetry, 2022), Firecracker Award, Balcones Poetry Prize, Quill and Ink, Paterson Poetry Prize, and IPPY Award nominee *Messengers of the Macabre* [co-written with David Davies] (Audience Askew, 2022), *Apprenticed to the Night* (UniVerse Press, 2023), and *Felones de Se: Poems about Suicide* (Ukiyoto Publishing, 2023).

Ngo Binh Anh Khoa is a teacher of English in Ho Chi Minh City, Vietnam. In his free time, he enjoys daydreaming, reading, and occasionally writing poetry for personal entertainment. His speculative poems have appeared in NewMyths.com, *Heroic Fantasy Quarterly, The Audient Void,* and other venues.

Manuel Pérez-Campos of Bayamón, Puerto Rico is a long-time poet in the tradition of the weird, with work published in several venues.

Carl E. Reed is currently employed as a call center agent at a retail fixtures company just outside Chicago. His poetry has been published in

The Iconoclast, Spectral Realms, Black Petals, and *Deathlehem: Holiday Horrors;* short stories in *Black Gate, newWitch, Sci-Fi Lampoon, Penumbra, Eldritch Tales,* and elsewhere. He is a member of Frank Coffman's Weird Poets Society. *Dark Matter,* a collection of his short stories and poetry, will be released in early 2024 by Hippocampus Press.

Geoffrey Reiter is Associate Professor and Coordinator of Literature at Lancaster Bible College. He is also an Associate Editor at the website *Christ and Pop Culture,* where he frequently writes about weird horror and dark fantasy. As a scholar of weird fiction, Reiter has published academic articles on such authors as Arthur Machen, Bram Stoker, Clark Ashton Smith, and William Peter Blatty. His poetry has previously appeared in *Spectral Realms* and *Star*Line,* and his fiction has appeared in *Penumbra* and *The Mythic Circle.*

Silvatiicus Riddle was nominated for the 2023 Rhysling Award for his poem "Exulansis," which appeared in the penultimate issue of *Liquid Imagination.* He is a dark fantasy and speculative fiction writer from New York City who hosts a glaring of chthonic gods disguised as cats, a hoard of books, and all his imaginary friends. He studied English and Literature at Kingsborough. He has appeared in *Abyss & Apex, Dreams & Nightmares, Enchanted Living,* and *Spectral Realms.*

Ann K. Schwader lives and writes in Colorado. Her newest collection, Unquiet Stars, is now out from Weird House Press. Two of her earlier collections, *Wild Hunt of the Stars* (Sam's Dot, 2010) and *Dark Energies* (P'rea Press, 2015), were Bram Stoker Award Finalists. In 2018, she received the Science Fiction and Fantasy Poetry Association's Grand Master award. She is also a two-time Rhysling Award winner.

A career retrospective of **Darrell Schweitzer**'s short fiction was published by PS Publishing in two volumes in 2020. A veritable flood of Schweitzeriana is soon to follow from various publishers in the next year or so, including a new Lovecraftian anthology, *Shadows out of Time* (PS), *The Best of Weird Tales: The 1920s* (Centipede Press), *The Best of Weird Tales 1924* (with John Betancourt, Wildside Press), a new story collection, *The Children of Chorazin* (Hippocampus), and two further volumes of author interviews (Wildside). He was co-editor of *Weird Tales* between 1988 and 2007.

Claire Smith writes about other worlds: fairy tale, folklore, mythology, and more. Her work has been featured in a number of journals and anthologies, including earlier issues of *Spectral Realms, Ink, Sweat & Tears, Strange Horizons,* and *Illumen*. She is currently reading for a Ph.D. in Humanities at the University of Gloucestershire, specializing in poetry. She lives in Gloucestershire, UK, with her husband, the writer Oliver Smith, and their spoilt Tonkinese cat, Ishtar.

Oliver Smith is an artist and writer from Cheltenham, Gloucestershire, UK. His poetry has appeared in *Dreams & Nightmares, Eye to the Telescope, Illumen, Mirror Dance, Rivet, Spectral Realms, Star*Line,* and *Weirdbook*. His collection of stories, *Stars Beneath the Ships,* was published by Ex Occidente Press in 2017, and many of his previously anthologized stories and poems are collected in *Basilisk Soup and Other Fantasies*. Oliver is studying for a Ph.D. in Creative Writing.

Jay Sturner is a writer, poet, and naturalist from the Chicago suburbs. He is the author of several books of poetry and a collection of short stories. His writing has appeared in such publications as the *Magazine of Fantasy & Science Fiction, Not One of Us, Space & Time, Star*Line,* and previous issues of *Spectral Realms*. In addition to being a writer, Sturner is also a professional bird walk leader.

DJ Tyrer is the person behind Atlantean Publishing and has been published in *The Rhysling Anthology,* issues of *Cyäegha, The Horrorzine, Scifaikuest, Sirens Call, Star*Line, Tigershark,* and *The Yellow Zine*. The e-chapbook *One Vision* is available from Tigershark Publishing. *SuperTrump* and *A Wuhan Whodunnit* are available for download from Atlantean Publishing.

Don Webb teaches horror writing for UCLA Extension and has been a top-rated instructor since 2004. He has been a member of Temple of Set for thirty-three years and written a great deal of esoterica such as *Energy Magick of the Vampyre*. In other words, he really does a cult following.

Andrew White lives in the mountains of North Carolina, where he jots down a poem from time to time. He derives inspiration from the mystical, the mythological, and all things Gothic/Lovecraftian. Andrew loves nature, his family, and black metal. A handful of his poems have been published, mostly in *Spectral Realms*.

Steven Withrow's poems appear in *Spectral Realms, Asimov's Science Fiction, and Dreams & Nightmares*. His poem "The Sun Ships," from an Elgin Award–nominated collection of the same title, was nominated for a 2016 Rhysling Award from the Science Fiction & Fantasy Poetry Association. His most recent solo collection is *The Bedlam Philharmonic*. His collection with Frank Coffman, *The Exorcised Lyric*, contains "Toward Solstice Station," a nominee for the 2022 Rhysling Award. He lives on Cape Cod.

Lee Clark Zumpe, an entertainment editor with Tampa Bay Newspapers, earned his bachelor's degree in English at the University of South Florida. He began writing poetry and fiction in the early 1990s. His work has regularly appeared in a variety of literary journals and genre magazines over the last few decades.

www.ingramcontent.com/pod-product-compliance
Lightning Source LLC
Chambersburg PA
CBHW060811050426
42449CB00008B/1631